WHERE LOVE STILL LINGERS

Poetry, Reflection, and The Healing Power of Words

Athena Rayne Kostas

Table of Contents

Introduction	01
Chapter 1: Rage Against the Unfairness	02
Chapter 2: The What-Ifs That Haunt Me	09
Chapter 3: Alone in a Crowded Room	16
Chapter 4: When Memories Hurt and Heal	24
Chapter 5: What Now? Finding Meaning After Loss	30
Chapter 6: Love Doesn't End	40
Chapter 7: A Moment of Light	49
Chapter 8: Becoming Someone New	56
Chapter 9: What Grief Has Taught Me	63
Chapter 10: Grief and Life, Hand in Hand	71
Chapter 11: To Those Who Walk This Path	78
Chapter 12: Creating Through Grief	86
Chapter 13: Carrying Love Forward	94
Additional Journal Prompts for Reflection	101
Acknowledgment	106
About the Author	107

INTRODUCTION

Grief is deeply personal. No two people experience it the same way, and there is no right or wrong way to process loss. For me, writing has been a powerful tool—a way to give my grief a voice, to untangle my emotions, and to hold onto love even through pain.

Throughout this book, you'll find journal prompts at the end of each chapter. These prompts are here as a guide—not as something you have to do, but as something you can turn to if and when you feel ready.

Some people may choose to write their thoughts in a separate journal, while others may simply reflect on the questions in their mind. There is no pressure to respond to every prompt, and there are no rules for how you should engage with them. This is your journey.

Whether you write a single word, a poem, or nothing at all, my hope is that these prompts will provide gentle guidance, validation, and space to explore your grief in whatever way feels right for you.

Chapter One

Rage Against The Unfairness

Grief is not just sorrow—it is fury. It is the fire that burns beneath the weight of loss, the raw and unrelenting anger at the world for allowing something so senseless to happen. It is the screaming voice in my head demanding, Why him? Why this way? Why does my son get a life sentence in the grave while the one who took him gets to walk free in a few short years?

When my son was killed, the grief was immediate, but the rage came soon after. It crept in slowly at first—an ember in the pit of my stomach—but it grew, feeding on every injustice, every reminder that life had moved on for others while I remained frozen in pain. The world expected me to grieve quietly, to mourn in a way that was palatable and socially acceptable. But how could I? How could I sit still when the very fabric of my reality had been ripped apart?

I wanted justice. I wanted answers. I wanted to scream, to destroy something, to make the universe feel a fraction of what I felt. But there was no way to undo what had been done. That's when I turned to writing. Poetry became my battleground, my way of giving form to the rage that threatened to consume me.

Severed Thread

Atropos, why? A question rings,
Across the silent, mournful strings
Of hearts that ache, and eyes that weep,
For slumber now, so deathly deep.

My boy, whose laughter filled the air,
Whose dreams were bright beyond compare,
Whose life, a sunrise, barely dawned,
By your sharp shears, so cruelly drawn.
He had a future, bold and bright,
A path to walk, bathed in the light,
Of sunlit days and moonlit nights,
A tapestry of pure delights.
But you, O Fate, with callous hand,
Did sever swift, across the land,
The fragile thread, so finely spun,
Before, his race was barely run.

◆ ◆ ◆

Tisiphone: Fury's Flame

I am Tisiphone, hear my cry,
Born of wrath where shadows lie.
Blood-stained hands, a vengeful gaze,
I walk the path of fury's blaze.

No plea can bend my iron will,
No tear can make my rage stand still.
For every life unjustly slain,
I rise, I hunt, I bring the pain.

Justice calls with fire and steel,
A debt in blood that fate must seal.
I am Tisiphone, fear my name—
For murder's echo fuels my flame.

❖❖❖

Anger is a natural part of grief, especially when loss comes through violence. But society often tells us to suppress it, to move past it quickly. We're told that anger is destructive, that it's not "productive." But for those of us who have lost someone in a senseless way, anger is inevitable. It's a sign of love, of injustice, of the part of us that refuses to accept what happened.

What matters is what we do with that anger. If we hold it in, it festers, poisoning us from the inside. If we lash out, we risk hurting ourselves and those around us. But if we express it, if we give it a voice through writing, art, or music, we take control. We let it out in a way that doesn't destroy us.

Poetry became my outlet. In words, I could scream. I could rage. I could make my fury known. I could let my grief be as loud as it needed to be—without apology.

If you feel this anger, know that you are not alone. Your pain is valid. Your fury is valid. And you deserve a place to release it.

Journal Prompts & Exercises

- Write a letter to the person or force responsible for your loss—say everything you've never said.
- If your grief took the form of a mythical being (like the Furies), how would it look?
- Create something that expresses your anger—don't hold back.

Chapter Two
The What-Ifs That Haunt Me

Guilt is grief's cruel companion. It whispers in the quiet moments, in the sleepless nights, in the spaces where love and loss collide. It asks impossible questions—What if I had done something differently? What if I had been there? What if I could have stopped it?—knowing full well that there are no answers.

When I lost my son, grief shattered me, but guilt was the weight that kept me down. Even though I knew, logically, that I wasn't responsible for what happened, my heart refused to believe it. I replayed the past over and over, searching for a moment where fate could have been rewritten. I wondered if I had failed him somehow. If I had missed a sign. If I had done enough.

I know now that guilt is a liar, but that doesn't mean it's easy to silence. It lingers, twisting itself into grief, making the loss even heavier to carry. The only way I've found to loosen its grip is through words. Writing forces guilt into the open, stripping it of its power. Poetry lets me take my pain and shape it into something I can hold—something real, but no longer just mine to bear.

What If

What if I was there, in that fateful hour,
To shield you from shadows, to call on my power?
What if my arms could have wrapped you so tight,
To keep you from danger that lurked in the night?

What if I had listened, just a little bit more,
If I had been present, if I'd gone through that door?
What if I was stronger, a better guide too,
Would the night have been different, would I still have you?

Echoes of silence now fill every room,
Each creak of the floor brings the weight of the gloom.
The whispers of "what if" dance round in my head,
A tormenting chorus for the child that is dead.

I walk through the memories, each laughter a blade,
Each joyful reminder now seems like a trade—
For hours spent wishing I'd changed just one thing,
To alter your fate, to halt the cruel sting.

Yet here I sit stranded in shadows of doubt,
Living with questions, a heart full of grief.
Could I have prevented the loss that I mourned?
In a world full of answers, why do I feel scorned?

But love, it still lingers, in every sweet sigh,
Though you're gone from my arms, our bond won't comply.
I carry your spirit, though plagued by the night,
In the quiet of memory, you still shine so bright.

◆ ◆ ◆

Guilt is one of the most isolating emotions in grief because it makes us feel like we're carrying a secret burden that no one else can understand. But the truth is, almost everyone who has lost someone—especially to a sudden or violent death—feels it in some way.

We question what we could have done differently. We punish ourselves with impossible scenarios, as if imagining a different outcome could somehow change the past. But guilt is not justice. It does not bring back the one we lost, nor does it honor their memory. It only deepens the wound.

The challenge is learning to let go—not of love, not of remembrance, but of the false belief that we had the power to change what was never in our control.

For me, writing has been one of the only ways to release guilt's grip. By putting my thoughts onto the page, I take them out of my head, where they echo endlessly. I invite you to do the same.

Journal Prompts & Exercises

- The Unfinished Conversation – If you could have one more conversation with your loved one, what would you say? Write it as if they were right in front of you. Let yourself be honest, raw, and unfiltered.
- What Would You Say to a Friend? – If someone you love was carrying the same guilt you feel, what would you tell them? Write yourself that same advice, as if you were speaking to your best friend.

- The Reality Check – Write down the things you blame yourself for. Then, next to each one, write an objective truth. For example:
    - "I should have known." → There was no way I could have known.
    - "I should have done more." → I did the best I could with what I knew at the time.

Chapter Three

Alone in a Crowded Room

Grief is lonely—not just because of the loss itself, but because of how the world responds to it. Or, more often, how it doesn't.

When my son died, I expected people to reach out. I thought they would check in, offer comfort, sit with me in my pain. But instead, they disappeared. Maybe they didn't know what to say. Maybe they were too caught up in their own lives. Maybe my grief made them uncomfortable. Whatever the reason, I found myself utterly alone.

No calls. No texts. No one showing up at my door. The silence was deafening. It made me wonder—was my pain invisible? Did no one care? Or did they just not want to deal with it?

The truth is, grief isolates you in ways you never expect.

Not only do you lose the person you love, but you lose the support you thought would be there. You lose the version of yourself that existed before. You lose the ability to move through the world the way you once did.

I carried my grief alone, not because I wanted to, but because I had no other choice. And in that loneliness, I turned to writing. Poetry became the space where I could speak without being ignored. The page didn't turn away. The words didn't leave me behind.

Hollow Veneer

In moments when the world collapsed,
And grief's shadows over me lapsed,
The faces once familiar, fade,
In the depths of sorrow, I'm left betrayed.

Those I held close, like threads unwind,
Their absence sharp, their silence unkind.
In the darkest hours, they disappear,
Leaving behind a hollow veneer.

♦♦♦

Empty Spaces

In shadows deep, my heart does ache,
A laugh once bright, now silence wakes.
Each step I take, the echo found,
Of memories lost, in grief profound.

Day blends to night, a heavy shroud,
Loneliness whispers, painfully loud.
A void so vast, where love once shone,
In empty spaces, I walk alone.

♦♦♦

Grief is isolating, not just because people don't always know what to say, but because it changes the way we see the world. When you've lost someone, everything looks different. You feel different. And that difference can make it hard to connect with others, even those who care about you.

Loneliness in grief isn't just about being physically alone—it's about feeling emotionally disconnected. You might sit in a room full of people and still feel like no one sees you, like the person you were before loss is gone, and no one recognizes who you are now.

That's why creative expression—writing, music, art—can be so powerful. It gives us a way to communicate when words fail. It allows us to express our pain without needing permission or understanding from others. It reminds us that even in loneliness, our emotions still have a place to go.

If you feel alone in your grief, know that you're not truly alone. Others have walked this path. Others have felt this same hollow ache. And while no one can take your grief away, you don't have to carry it in silence.

Journal Prompts & Exercises

- A Letter to the Void – Write a letter about your grief to someone who won't judge—whether it's your lost loved one, a higher power, or even just an empty sky. Let yourself say everything you've been holding inside.

- The Room of Loneliness – Imagine your loneliness as a physical space. What does it look like? Is it empty? Crowded but silent? What colors, textures, or sounds exist there? Describe it in detail.
- A Doorway to Connection – If you could open a door and find one person waiting on the other side who truly understood your grief, who would it be? What would they say to you?

Chapter Four

When Memories Hurt and Heal

Memories are heavy. Some days, they are all I have left of my son, and I cling to them like a lifeline. Other days, they feel like daggers, sharp reminders of what I will never have again. The laughter, the small moments, the sound of his voice—they bring both comfort and pain, love and loss, healing and heartbreak.

In the beginning, the memories were unbearable. They came in waves, crashing over me when I least expected them. A song playing in a store, a scent in the air, a place we used to go. Each one sent me spiraling, reminding me of what was stolen from me. I wanted to hold onto those moments, but at the same time, I couldn't face them without breaking.

With time, I learned that memories don't have to be just pain. They can be a way to honor, to remember, to keep the love alive. Writing about my son—about the moments we shared, about who he was—helped me find a way to carry him with me, rather than just mourn his absence.

His Bright, Brief Song

The scent of pine, the campfire's glow,
My son beside me, watching slow.
The embers dance, a fiery show,
As childhood memories softly flow.

He loved the lake and its gentle roar,
His laughter echoing from shore to shore.
A boundless spirit, forevermore,
A light that shines, I can't ignore.

Two wheels, a path, a summer's day,
Side by side, we'd ride and play.
Those carefree moments fade away,
Yet vivid still, in my heart's display.

The pain of loss, a heavy weight,
A wound that time cannot abate.
Yet through the tears, I celebrate
The love we shared, before it was late.

For in the dance of life and loss,
A bittersweet and tender cross,
I'd choose it all, whatever the cost,
To hold those memories, never lost.

♦♦♦

Memories are complicated in grief. In the beginning, they can feel like torture—a reminder of everything that's missing. But over time, they can also become a source of connection, a way to hold onto the person we love.

It's okay if your memories hurt. It's okay if they bring tears instead of comfort. Grief doesn't follow a straight path, and neither do the emotions that come with remembering. The important thing is to let yourself feel, to give those memories a place to exist—not just in pain, but in love.

Creative expression, whether through writing, music, or art, allows us to engage with memories in a way that is both healing and meaningful. When we put them into words, we make sure they don't fade. When we create something from them, we find a way to hold onto the love that will never leave us.

Journal Prompts & Exercises

- A Memory Worth Keeping – Write about a memory of your loved one that brings you joy. Describe it in vivid detail—what you saw, heard, felt. Let yourself relive it on the page.
- A Moment I Wish I Could Relive – Is there a memory you hold onto that feels unfinished? Write about it as if you were back in that moment, saying or doing everything you wish you had.
- Turning Pain into Art – Take a difficult memory and express it creatively. Write a poem, paint an image, or compose a song that captures the emotions it brings.

Chapter Five
What Now?
Finding Meaning After Loss

When my son was taken from me, my world shattered. Not just my daily life, not just my heart, but my entire understanding of existence. How could something so cruel happen? How could someone so full of life, with so much ahead of him, just be gone?

I searched for meaning in the aftermath. I wanted answers—why did this happen? Was it fate? Was it random? Was there some kind of lesson I was supposed to take from this unbearable pain? But there were no answers, only silence. And in that silence, I felt lost.

People often try to offer meaning in grief. Everything happens for a reason. He's in a better place. You'll grow stronger from this. But those words felt hollow, even cruel. I didn't want to find meaning in my son's death—I wanted him here, living the life he was meant to have.

But over time, I learned that meaning isn't something that just appears. It isn't found in clichés or empty reassurances. It's something we create for ourselves. And for me, writing became part of that process. When I put my pain into poetry, I wasn't just drowning in grief—I was doing something with it. I was making sure my son's name, his love, and his impact didn't just disappear.

I don't know if I'll ever fully understand why this happened.

But I do know that I can still choose how I carry my grief. And in that choice, in that creation, I find something close to meaning.

The meaning we make

The world went dim, a sudden night,
A star extinguished, robbed of light.
My heart, a shattered, fragile thing,
Could barely hear the robin sing.

The days crawled by, a heavy chain,
Each moment etched with endless pain.
The laughter gone, the gentle touch,
A silent void, I loved so much.

The sun refused to shine its best,
The flowers wilted, in my breast
A hollow ache, a constant dread,
A future painted shades of grey instead.

I stumbled through a shadowed land,
A broken spirit, hand in hand
With grief, a cruel and constant friend,
Whose bitter solace knew no end.

I searched for answers, sought a sign,
A whisper from beyond the line
That separates the living here,
From loved ones lost, year after year.

I spoke their name in silent plea,
A yearning for what used to be.
The memories, like fragile glass,
Would shatter as the moments pass.

But slowly, softly, in the gloom,
A tiny spark began to bloom.
A memory, a gentle face,
A smile recalled, a warm embrace.

It whispered hope, a gentle breeze,
That stirred the leaves of weary trees.
And in that hope, a strength arose,
To soften grief, to soothe the woes.

I found it not in sudden might,
But in the quiet of the night.
In simple things, the morning dew,
The colors bright, the sky so blue.

The birdsong sweet, the gentle rain,
Soothed weary heart and eased the pain.
I learned to breathe, to live again,
To find the sun, to dull the pain.

The tears still fall, a gentle stream,
A testament to what has been.
But through the tears, a light appears,
A fragile hope that conquers fears.

I plant a tree, a symbol strong,
To mark the place where love belonged.
And as it grows, so does my heart,
Renewed, reborn, a brand new start.

The journey long, the path unclear,
But hope's soft light dispels all fear.

Though shadows linger, I now know,
That love endures, even in woe.

The meaning found, not in the end,
But in the love that will transcend.
A love that binds, a love that stays,
Through darkest nights and brightest days.
And though the pain may never cease,

I find a comfort, a release.
In memories shared, a gentle hand,
A love that guides me, through the land.
The land of hope, where life's reborn,

A new beginning, met at morn.
And in that dawn, I find my peace,
My journey's end, my heart's release.

♦ ♦ ♦

Grief makes us question everything. It shakes the foundation of what we believe about life, death, and purpose. Some people find comfort in faith, believing their loved one is still with them in some way. Others struggle with the randomness of it all, feeling like nothing makes sense anymore. Wherever you fall, those questions are part of the journey.

Meaning isn't always about finding an answer—it's about what we do with our grief. Some find purpose in advocacy, in honoring their loved one, in creative expression, or in small daily acts of remembrance.

There is no "right" way to make sense of loss. But if you're searching for meaning, know that you're not alone. And that sometimes, meaning isn't about understanding—it's about creating.

Journal Prompts & Exercises

- What Would Meaning Look Like for You? – If you could create your own sense of meaning after loss, what would it be? Would it be through action, creation, remembrance? Write about how you'd like to honor your loved one.
- What Do You Believe Now? – Has grief changed your views on life, fate, or the afterlife? Write about how your beliefs have shifted since your loss.

- If You Could Ask One Question and Get an Answer – Imagine you could ask the universe, fate, or a higher power one question about your loss and get a real answer. What would you ask? How do you think the answer would change you?

Chapter Six

Love Doesn't End

When my son died, I feared that over time, I would lose pieces of him. That his voice would fade in my mind, that his laughter would grow distant, that the world would move forward and leave his memory behind. The thought of that terrified me.

But I've learned that love doesn't end when someone dies. It doesn't vanish with time. It doesn't fade just because the world keeps turning. Love is carried—it lives in the memories we hold, in the stories we tell, in the ways we choose to honor those we've lost.

For me, that means creating space in my life where his presence still feels near. On his birthday, I make his favorite food and remember the joy he found in it. In the quiet moments, I sit in the memorial garden I made for him, a cup of coffee in my hands, letting the warmth and stillness bring me closer to him. These small rituals aren't grand gestures—they are simple, everyday ways of saying: I remember. I love you. You are still with me.

I still speak his name. I still think of him in quiet moments. I still feel his presence in the things he loved—the scent of pine, the sound of the lake, the songs that remind me of him. And in those moments, I know that love isn't something death can take away. It stays, woven into who I am, guiding me forward even in my grief.

I may have lost him physically, but I will never lose the love we shared. And in that, he is never truly gone.

Eternal Echoes

In the quiet of the morning light,
Where shadows dance and hearts take flight,
I feel his presence, soft and near,
A whispered love that calms my fear.

Though he has traveled far away,
In realms where sunlight warms the day,
I carry him in every breath,
His laughter mingles with the rest.

I will speak his name, a sacred sound,
In every moment he's still around,
In joy's embrace and sorrow's sigh,
He's in the stars that fill the sky.

Happy memories, like gentle streams,
Flow through my heart, igniting dreams,
Of days we shared, the laughter, the play,
In the tapestry of love that will never fray.

Hope blooms like flowers in springtime's grace,
In the tender shadows, I still find his place,
A garden of peace where spirits align,
Where love transcends the limits of time.

So I will hold him, forever dear,
In every heartbeat, in every tear,
For though the world feels dim and stark,
His light remains, a guiding spark.

I will speak his name, let it ring clear,
In the fabric of my days, he will always be near,
For love knows no bounds, and death is not the end,
In the echoes of my heart, my son, my friend.

♦♦♦

There's a common idea that grief is something you "get over." That eventually, you move on, let go, and leave it behind. But that's not how grief works. You don't stop loving someone just because they're no longer here.

Carrying love forward doesn't mean pretending the pain isn't there. It means allowing both love and loss to exist together. It means finding ways to keep their presence in your life—through memories, through honoring them, through the simple act of remembering.

For me, that means embracing the things that remind me of my son. Drinking coffee in the garden I created for him, celebrating his birthday with his favorite food, speaking his name without hesitation. These acts don't just keep his memory alive—they keep my love for him alive.

Some people create traditions to honor their loved ones. Others keep their memory alive through storytelling, through creativity, or through small rituals that keep them close. There is no right or wrong way to do this—only what feels right for you.

Love doesn't end. And because of that, neither do the people we carry in our hearts.

Journal Prompts & Exercises

- Speaking Their Name – Write about a moment when you felt your loved one's presence, whether through a memory, a sign, or a simple feeling.

- A Ritual of Remembrance – If you could create a way to honor your loved one, what would it be? A yearly tradition? A creative project? Describe how you would keep their memory alive.
- If They Could Speak to You Now – Imagine your loved one could send you a message today. What do you think they would say? Write it as if they were speaking directly to you.

Chapter Seven

A Moment of Light

For a long time, I didn't think healing was possible. The idea of feeling better felt like a betrayal—like moving forward meant leaving my son behind. The pain had become so much a part of me that I couldn't imagine existing without it.

But then, one day, something shifted. It wasn't dramatic. It wasn't a grand moment of transformation. It was something small. Maybe it was the way the sun felt on my skin after days of staying inside. Maybe it was a song that made me smile instead of cry. Maybe it was simply a moment when the grief wasn't all-consuming—when I could breathe without the weight of sorrow crushing my chest.

For me, that moment came in the form of a crow.

Before my son died, I greeted the crows in my yard every morning, calling them my crow friends. But when grief took over, I stopped noticing them. The world had lost its color, and even the small joys that once made up my day had disappeared.

Until one morning, when I saw a crow in my yard again. Without thinking, I smiled and said, "Hello, my crow friend." And in return, it cawed back at me.

It was a small thing, barely a moment, but it was enough.

Enough to remind me that I was still here. That healing isn't about erasing pain, but about allowing light to slip through the cracks.

The Crow's Return

The silence echoed, a void so profound,

The crows, once friends, no longer found.

In the depths of grief, their calls unheard,

My heart, a fortress, remained unstirred.

But then, one day, a familiar sight,

The crow returned, a glimmer of light.

A moment of reconnection, a spark ignite,

Healing's journey, a gradual delight.

I met its gaze, both knowing and wise,

A flicker of life behind weary eyes.

Softly I whispered, "Hello, my crow friend,"

And with a caw, it called back again.

Not sudden, this path to mend the soul,

But in these moments, the heart grows whole.

A familiar joy, a comfort so true,

Reminding me, life's beauty shines anew.

♦♦♦

Healing isn't about "getting over" loss. It's not a finish line we cross. It's about learning to carry grief in a way that doesn't break us.

The first glimpse of healing often comes in the smallest of moments—ones that we barely notice at first. It could be laughing at something unexpected. It could be feeling warmth instead of numbness. It could be picking up a creative passion again, even if just for a moment.

These moments don't mean we are done grieving. They don't mean we've forgotten. They simply mean that love and loss can coexist with life. And that even in the depths of grief, light still finds its way in.

Journal Prompts & Exercises

- A Small Moment of Light – Think of a time when your grief felt a little lighter, even for just a second. Describe that moment in detail—where were you? What did you feel?
- Permission to Heal – Write a letter to yourself, giving yourself permission to experience moments of peace and joy without guilt.
- A kindness Remembered – Write about a time when someone showed you kindness during your grief. What did they do? How did it make you feel? How has the moment stayed with you?

Chapter Eight

Becoming Someone New

Grief changes everything. It doesn't just take away the person you love—it takes away the version of you that existed before the loss. I used to think I knew who I was. I had dreams, routines, and a sense of stability in my life. But when my son was taken from me, that version of myself shattered.

For a long time, I didn't recognize the person in the mirror. I felt like a stranger in my own life—walking through familiar places, but nothing felt the same. The things that once brought me joy seemed hollow. My sense of purpose was lost. I wasn't the person I used to be, but I didn't know who I was becoming, either.

But slowly, I started to understand that the old me was gone—not just because of grief, but because I had changed. And not all of that change was loss.

The old me dreamed of writing a book, but I never even got started. I let fear hold me back—fear that it wouldn't be good enough, that people wouldn't like it. But after enduring the worst thing that could ever happen to a parent, those fears seem trivial now. The new me is brave enough to share my words. The new me knows that life is too short to stay silent. The new me is writing.

I will never be the same person I was before my loss. But I am still here. And though I am different, I am finding strength in the person I am becoming.

Phoenix Reborn

A part of me turned to ash that day,

scorched by sorrow, swept away.

The world I knew, the self I was,

lost beneath grief's cruelest touch.

I burned, I crumbled, I fell apart,

embers smouldering in my heart.

The weight of loss, the shroud of pain,

left me wondering who remained.

But from the ruins, flames arise,

a spark, a flicker in my eyes.

Not untouched, not free from scars,

but stronger now than once I was.

I am still me—compassion's fire,

a heart that aches, a soul that tires.

But fear has loosened, lost its chain,

for I have walked through death and flame.

No longer silenced, no longer small,

I spread my wings—I will not fall.

For though I grieve, though I have mourned,

I rise again. I am reborn.

♦♦♦

Grief reshapes identity in ways we never expect. It changes how we see the world, our relationships, and even ourselves. Some people find that they no longer relate to the same friends. Others realise their values and priorities have shifted. For many, grief brings both loss and transformation.

It's okay to feel like you don't know who you are anymore. It's okay to mourn not just your loved one, but also the version of yourself that existed before. But it's also okay to grow—to allow yourself to become someone new, shaped by love, loss, and resilience.

Who you are now is not a lesser version of who you were before. You are someone who has endured, who has learned, who carries love even through pain. And that is a person worth embracing.

Journal Prompts & Exercises

- Who Was I Before? – Write about who you were before your loss. What were your dreams, your values, the things that defined you? How have they changed?
- Who Am I Now? – Describe the person you are becoming. What qualities do you carry now that you didn't before? What parts of yourself still feel like you?
- A Letter to My Past Self – If you could speak to the version of yourself before your loss, what would you say? What do you wish they knew about grief, survival, and transformation?

Chapter Nine

What Grief Has Taught Me

Grief is a teacher—one I never wanted, but one I could not avoid. It has reshaped the way I see the world, the way I connect with others, and the way I understand myself.

One of the first lessons I learned is that no two people grieve the same way. In the beginning, people tried to tell me how I should grieve—what I should do, how I should feel. But grief doesn't follow a script. It is deeply personal, and what works for one person may not work for another. I've learned that the best thing we can do for someone grieving is not to assume we know what they need, but to ask. And if they don't know? Just be there. Presence matters more than words.

I also learned that boundaries are crucial—especially when grief is public. Losing someone to homicide comes with layers of trauma that few people understand. The media, the legal system, and even well-meaning acquaintances can turn grief into something invasive. I had to learn to protect myself, to say no, to step back from conversations that drained me. Setting boundaries isn't selfish—it's survival.

And perhaps one of the hardest lessons for me was understanding that grief cannot be carried alone. I have always been someone who handles things on my own. But traumatic grief—especially the kind that comes with fear, anxiety, and the aftershocks of violence—requires support. I had to learn how to lean on others, to let people in, to accept that I needed a system of care. And that, in itself, was a form of strength.

I am still learning. Grief is an ongoing lesson. But these truths have shaped me, helping me navigate a world forever changed.

What Grief Whispered to Me

Grief is a long winding path, full of thorns and tears,
The lessons learned are etched deep through the passing years.
In shadows where the silence lies, I found a fragile grace,
Each moment that I held so close, adorned with love's embrace.

The echoes of lost laughter weave through every hurtful night,
Yet in the depths of sorrow's clutch, I learned to seek the light.
For in the darkest valleys, where despair can take its throne,
I glimpsed the strength within my heart, a light I could call home.

I've learned that love endures beyond what eyes can see or touch,
Through every aching memory, it teaches me so much.
Connections forged in sorrow bloom, like flowers through the frost,
Reminding me that every tear still holds the love I keep.

So though the journey's heavy, and the road may seem unkind,
Grief has taught me to embrace the beauty I can find.
With every wipe of tear-stained cheeks, I rise to meet each day,
For in the heart of grief, I've found a wiser way to stay.

♦♦♦

Grief forces us to see the world differently. It teaches lessons that we never asked for, but ones that become essential to survival.

Everyone grieves differently. There is no right or wrong way. The best thing we can do for others is to honor their process, not impose our own.

Boundaries are necessary. Protecting your space, energy, and emotions is part of healing.

Traumatic grief carries unique weight. Fear, anxiety, and emotional exhaustion are real. A support system isn't just helpful—it's critical.

Strength doesn't mean doing it alone. True strength is knowing when to lean on others.

These lessons have shaped the way I move through grief. They are hard-won truths, but they have helped me find my way through.

Journal Prompts & Exercises

- What Has Grief Taught You? – Reflect on the lessons you've learned from your own loss. How has grief changed the way you see life, love, or yourself?
- Setting Boundaries in Grief – Write about a time when you needed to set a boundary while grieving. What happened? How did it make you feel?

- Supporting Others in Grief – If you could give advice to someone trying to help a grieving person, what would it be? What did you need most in your own grief?

Chapter Ten

Grief and Life, Hand in Hand

I used to think that grief had an ending—that one day, I would wake up, and the weight of loss would be gone. That time would heal me, that I would reach some point where I felt normal again. But that's not how grief works.

Grief doesn't disappear. It doesn't fade neatly into the past. It becomes a part of you. It lingers in unexpected moments—a familiar song, a scent in the air, an empty chair at the table. Some days, it feels light, like a shadow that follows me but doesn't overwhelm me. Other days, it feels just as heavy as the first moment I lost him.

But I have learned that I don't have to fight my grief. I don't have to outrun it or pretend it isn't there. Instead, I have learned to walk with it.

Grief is a companion I never wanted, but one I have come to understand. It reminds me of what I've lost, but also of what I still carry—the love, the memories, the pieces of my son that will always be with me.

I am not the same person I was before. My life is not the same. But I am still living. And that is enough.

A Tapestry in Time

I find the path is long,
Where shadows whisper softly,
And memories make me strong.

Each step I take beside it,
The weight, both light and dense,
A dance of sorrow's presence
And joy's quiet, vibrant sense.

The air is thick with longing,
Yet sunlight breaks the grey,
In moments stitched with laughter,
I learn to share the day.

With tears that flow like rivers,
I build a bridge to peace,
In sorrow's tender echo,
From joy, I claim my release.

So here I walk, undefeated,
In balance, heart of mine,
For grief and joy are woven,
A tapestry in time.

♦♦♦

Living with grief means accepting that it never fully goes away. It means learning how to carry it without letting it consume you. It means making space for both sorrow and joy, knowing that they can exist side by side.

Grief shows up in unexpected ways. It can be triggered by a song, a scent, or even just a quiet moment of reflection. Some days, it feels manageable. Other days, it feels like a wave crashing over you. Neither is wrong. Both are part of the journey.

But living with grief also means allowing yourself to experience life again. It means laughing without guilt, finding happiness in small moments, allowing yourself to feel without fear that you are forgetting.

Grief does not mean the absence of life. It means learning how to carry both love and loss at the same time.

Journal Prompts & Exercises

- A Day with Grief – Describe a day when grief felt present but didn't overwhelm you. What did it feel like? How did you carry it?
- Finding Joy Again – Write about a moment where you felt happiness after your loss. What was it like? Did you feel guilty? How did you allow yourself to experience it?
- If Grief Were a Companion – If grief was a person walking beside you, how would you describe them?

What would they say to you? How have they changed over time?

Chapter Eleven
To Those Who Walk This Path

If you are reading this and you are grieving, I want you to know—you are not alone. I know it may feel like you are. I know the weight of grief can be so isolating, so heavy, that it seems no one else in the world could possibly understand. But I promise you, you are not walking this road by yourself.

Grief is messy. It is unpredictable. Some days, you might feel numb. Other days, it will hit you like a tidal wave, knocking you to your knees. There is no right way to grieve, no timeline, no rulebook to follow. However you are feeling right now—it is okay. You are allowed to grieve in your own way, in your own time.

People will say things that hurt, even when they mean well. They will tell you to move on, to find closure, to be strong. They may try to offer words of comfort that feel empty or dismissive. But the truth is, grief isn't something you get over. It is something you learn to carry. And no one else gets to tell you how that journey should look.

I won't tell you that time heals all wounds. I won't say that one day, this will all be behind you. But I will tell you this—you will survive this. You will learn how to live with your grief. You will find small moments of light, even in the darkness. And you will carry the love you lost with you, always.

If no one has told you this yet: You are allowed to grieve. You are allowed to feel everything. And you are not alone.

Walking Together

(For those who walk this road with me, even in silence.)

Grief is a road, winding and steep,
Some days I run, some days I weep.
The path is dark, the air so still,
A weight I fear I'll carry still.

At first, I walk this road alone,
Each step is heavy, cold as stone.
The silence echoes, raw and deep,
A promise made, a love I keep.

But then, a whisper, soft yet true,
A voice that says, "I'm here with you."
I turn to see, through mist and shade,
Another soul, just as frayed.

We do not speak, no words are said,
Yet side by side, our grief is shared.
A knowing glance, a steady pace,
A hand outstretched, a touch of grace.

And though my sorrow does not cease,
I find in them a gentle peace.
For I am not alone, I see,
There are others here, walking with me.

♦♦♦

Grief is one of the hardest things a person can endure. It changes you. It reshapes your world. But if there is one thing I have learned, it is that you don't have to do it alone.

Your grief is your own. No one else can tell you how to grieve, how long it should take, or what healing should look like.

It is okay to ask for help. Whether it's a friend, a support group, or a therapist—leaning on others does not make you weak.

You are not broken. You are grieving because you loved. And that love still exists, even in loss.
Healing doesn't mean forgetting. Moving forward doesn't mean leaving your loved one behind—you carry them with you, always.

Grief is a path that none of us choose, but if you are walking it, please know—there are others walking it with you.

Journal Prompts & Exercises

- A Letter to Someone Who Doesn't Understand Grief – If you could explain your grief to someone who doesn't get it, what would you say? What do you wish they knew?
- What I Needed to Hear – Think back to the hardest days of your grief. What words would have comforted you most? Write them down as if speaking to yourself in that moment.

- Carrying Love Forward – How do you keep your loved one's memory alive? Write about the ways you still feel connected to them.

Chapter Twelve
Creating Through Grief

Grief is heavy. It fills the spaces of your mind, your body, your heart. In the early days of my loss, it felt impossible to put into words. The pain was too big, too consuming. But eventually, the words came—first as fragments, then as poems, then as something I could hold in my hands.

Writing became my way of surviving grief. It allowed me to process emotions too overwhelming to speak aloud. It gave me a place to pour my sorrow, my anger, my longing, my love. The page became a space where I could say all the things I couldn't say to the world.

For some, healing comes through painting, like my friend Roman, who turns his grief into art. For others, it comes through music—the right song at the right moment can break you open or stitch you back together. But for me, it has always been writing. Words have been my way through.

I have learned that creative expression is not about making something beautiful—it is about making something true. Grief is messy. Healing is messy. But in creativity, there is space to feel without judgment, to give grief a voice, to make sure our love and pain are seen, heard and remembered.

Lines of Loss, Lines of Love

When grief weighs heavy on the heart,
Writing becomes a healing art.
The words flow, a cathartic release,
Allowing emotions to find their peace.

Pen to paper, a canvas to paint,
Expressing thoughts that words can't taint.
Thoughts unspoken, now given a voice,
Transforming sorrow into a choice.

To process the pain, to let it unfold,
Writing's embrace, a story untold.
Emotions unleashed, no longer confined,
Healing the wounds of the troubled mind.

Through the act of writing, we find a way,
To navigate the darkest of days.
A path to understanding, a journey of grace,
As we learn to embrace the grief we face.

♦♦♦

Writing doesn't take grief away, but it gives it a place to go. It turns something invisible—pain, love, memory—into something real, something tangible.

Creative expression is powerful because it allows us to:

Release emotions: Writing lets us pour out the things we struggle to say aloud.

Find clarity: Putting grief into words helps untangle emotions and process what feels impossible.

Honor memories: Writing keeps the love alive, ensuring those we've lost are never forgotten.

Give grief a voice: When the world expects us to be silent in our sorrow, writing lets us speak.

Whether it's a journal entry, a poem, a letter to someone we've lost—writing offers a way forward. Not out of grief, but through it.

Journal Prompts & Exercises

- *A Letter to Your Loved One*: Write a letter to the person you lost. Tell them what you miss, what has changed, what you wish you could say.
- *The Shape of Your Grief:* If your grief had a form, what would it be? Describe it in detail. Is it a storm? A shadow? A river? A bird?

- *What Writing Has Given Me:*

    Reflect on how writing (or another form of creativity) has helped you process your emotions.

Chapter Thirteen

Carrying Love Forward

For a long time, I thought healing meant moving on. That eventually, I would reach a point where the pain would fade, where I could close this chapter of my life and start a new one. But I have learned that love doesn't end when life does.

My son is not here physically, but he is still a part of me. He is in the memories I hold close, in the lessons he taught me, in the love that will never fade. I carry him with me in the small moments—when I hear a song he loved, when I visit a place we shared, when I simply speak his name.

Carrying love forward means finding ways to honor those we've lost, not leaving them behind. It means allowing grief and joy to coexist, knowing that even in loss, love remains. It means giving ourselves permission to live—not because we have forgotten, but because love itself is a reason to keep going.

I will always miss my son. But I will also always love him. And that love will walk with me, every step of the way.

Where Love Still Lingers

You are not here, yet never far,
Your love still lingers where we are.
I carry you in morning light,
In songs we sang, in dreams at night.

In whispered prayers, in coffee warm,
In laughter shared, in love's true form.
I carry you in all I do,
My heart still beats with love for you.
The days may pass, the years may go,
But in my heart, your memory will grow.
Your smile, your laugh, your gentle touch,
These are the things I miss so much.
I find you in the sunset's glow,
The breeze that whispers, soft and low.
In nature's beauty, all around,
Your presence, there, can still be found.
Though you're not here, you're never gone,
Your spirit lives, it carries on.
In every moment, every breath,
I feel your love, beyond all death.
So I will cherish every day,
The time we had, the words we'd say.
And though my heart may sometimes ache,
I know, one day, we'll be awake.

Together, in that heavenly place,
Where I can see your shining face.
Until that day, I'll hold you near,
In my heart, my love, my son so dear.

♦♦♦

Carrying love forward means:

- *Keeping their memory alive:* Through stories, traditions, or simply speaking their name.
- *Allowing joy without guilt:* Grief doesn't mean we have to stay in pain forever.
- *Living in a way that honors them:* Taking what they taught us and continuing forward.
- *Understanding that love never ends:* The bond we have with those we've lost continues, even beyond this life.

Grief is not the end of love. It is proof that love existed. And love, real love, never fades.

Journal Prompts & Exercises

- A Legacy of Love – How do you continue to carry your loved one's memory with you? Write about the ways they remain a part of your life.
- If They Could See You Now – Imagine your loved one could send you a message today. What do you think they would say?
- Finding Meaning in Love – How has your loss changed the way you view love, life, and what truly matters?

Additional Journal Prompts for Reflection

Grief is not a linear journey—it ebbs and flows, revealing new emotions and insights over time. These prompts are here to support you as you continue to process your loss, honor your loved one, and find healing in your own way. Use them in moments of reflection, journaling, or whenever you feel the need to express your thoughts and emotions.

Processing Grief

- What is something you wish you could say to your loved one today?
- How has grief changed your daily routine or habits?
- Write about a moment when grief caught you off guard.
- Describe what "grief" feels like in your body.
- What are some of the hardest emotions you've faced in your grief?

Healing & Resilience

- What are some things that have helped you cope with loss?
- Write about a memory that brings both joy and sadness.
- Who in your life has supported you the most? How have they helped?

- How do you take care of yourself when grief feels overwhelming?
- What advice would you give to someone newly experiencing loss?

Hope & Transformation

- What does healing mean to you?
- Describe a moment when you felt a sense of peace or connection to your loved one.
- How has your perspective on life changed since your loss?
- What are some small things that bring you comfort?
- Imagine your loved one leaving you a message of encouragement—what might it say?

Acknowledgments

Writing this book has been both a journey of healing and an act of love. It would not have been possible without the support, encouragement, and presence of so many people.

To my son—This book is for you, because of you. Your love, your memory, and your light will always be with me. Every word I write carries a piece of you.

To my family—Thank you for standing beside me, lifting me up, and reminding me that I am never alone in this journey.

To Roman—For your unwavering support, for the quiet moments of understanding, and for reminding me that even in grief, we walk together.

To Julie—For your unwavering kindness and support. Your wisdom and compassion have made a difference in my journey, and I am deeply grateful.

And finally, to my readers—If you are holding this book in your hands, know that you are not alone. Thank you for allowing my words to be a part of your journey. My hope is that you find comfort, connection, and the reminder that love never fades.

About the Author

Athena Rayne Kostas is a writer and poet who uses words to process grief, healing, and love. After the tragic loss of her son, she turned to writing as a way to navigate the depths of sorrow and find a path forward. Through poetry and reflection, she shares her journey with the hope that others who are grieving will feel less alone.

She finds comfort in her family, especially her three sons, and in quiet moments spent honoring the memory of those she has lost. She believes that love endures beyond grief, and that writing can be a powerful tool for healing.

She lives in Winnipeg, Manitoba, where she continues to write and find meaning in everyday moments.

Where Love Still Lingers is her testament to the enduring power of love, even in the face of loss.

www.ingramcontent.com/pod-product-compliance
Lightning Source LLC
Chambersburg PA
CBHW030453010526
44118CB00011B/916